AUDIO ACCESS INCLUDED

CLARINET

T0087138

GREAT CLASSICAL THEMES

Audio Arrangements by Peter Deneff

To access audio visit:
www.halleonard.com/mylibrary

Enter Code
2875-3664-5690-9150

ISBN 978-1-5400-5036-6

Copyright © 2019 by HAL LEONARD LLC
International Copyright Secured All Rights Reserved

For all works contained herein:
Unauthorized copying, arranging, adapting, recording, Internet posting, public performance,
or other distribution of the music in this publication is an infringement of copyright.
Infringers are liable under the law.

Visit Hal Leonard Online at
www.halleonard.com

Contact us:
Hal Leonard
7777 West Bluemound Road
Milwaukee, WI 53213
Email: info@halleonard.com

In Europe, contact:
Hal Leonard Europe Limited
42 Wigmore Street
Marylebone, London, W1U 2RN
Email: info@halleonardeurope.com

In Australia, contact:
Hal Leonard Australia Pty. Ltd.
4 Lentara Court
Cheltenham, Victoria, 3192 Australia
Email: info@halleonard.com.au

CONTENTS

BLUE DANUBE WALTZ

Op. 314

CLARINET

By JOHANN STRAUSS, JR.

Copyright © 2019 by HAL LEONARD LLC
International Copyright Secured All Rights Reserved

CAN CAN

from ORPHEUS IN THE UNDERWORLD

CLARINET

By JACQUES OFFENBACH

Copyright © 2019 by HAL LEONARD LLC
International Copyright Secured All Rights Reserved

EINE KLEINE NACHTMUSIK

("Serenade")
(First Movement Theme)

CLARINET

By WOLFGANG AMADEUS MOZART

Copyright © 2019 by HAL LEONARD LLC
International Copyright Secured All Rights Reserved

f
mp
mp
f
f

GRAND MARCH

from AÏDA

CLARINET

By GIUSEPPE VERDI

Copyright © 2019 by HAL LEONARD LLC
International Copyright Secured All Rights Reserved

HABANERA
from CARMEN

CLARINET

By GEORGES BIZET

Copyright © 2019 by HAL LEONARD LLC
International Copyright Secured All Rights Reserved

HORNPIPE

from WATER MUSIC

CLARINET

By GEORGE FRIDERIC HANDEL

Copyright © 2019 by HAL LEONARD LLC
International Copyright Secured All Rights Reserved

HUNGARIAN DANCE NO. 5

CLARINET

By JOHANNES BRAHMS

Copyright © 2019 by HAL LEONARD LLC
International Copyright Secured All Rights Reserved

JESU, JOY OF MAN'S DESIRING

from CANTATA 147
BWV 147

CLARINET

By JOHANN SEBASTIAN BACH

Moderately slow

Flute

Play

mp

mf

f

2

mp

3

rit.

Copyright © 2017 by HAL LEONARD LLC
International Copyright Secured All Rights Reserved

LARGO

from SYMPHONY NO. 9 IN E MINOR
"FROM THE NEW WORLD"

CLARINET

By ANTONÍN DVOŘÁK

Copyright © 2005 by HAL LEONARD CORPORATION
International Copyright Secured All Rights Reserved

MORNING MOOD

from PEER GYNT

CLARINET

By EDVARD GRIEG

Copyright © 2019 by HAL LEONARD LLC
International Copyright Secured All Rights Reserved

ODE TO JOY

from SYMPHONY NO. 9 IN D MINOR

CLARINET

By LUDWIG VAN BEETHOVEN

Copyright © 2005 by HAL LEONARD CORPORATION
International Copyright Secured All Rights Reserved

THE SORCERER'S APPRENTICE

CLARINET

By PAUL DUKAS

Copyright © 2019 by HAL LEONARD LLC
International Copyright Secured All Rights Reserved

2
1.
2.
mp
ff

SPRING

from THE FOUR SEASONS

CLARINET

By ANTONIO VIVALDI

Copyright © 2019 by HAL LEONARD LLC
International Copyright Secured All Rights Reserved

THE SURPRISE SYMPHONY

from SYMPHONY NO. 94, SECOND MOVEMENT THEME

CLARINET

By FRANZ JOSEPH HAYDN

Copyright © 2019 by HAL LEONARD LLC
International Copyright Secured All Rights Reserved

WILLIAM TELL OVERTURE

Theme

CLARINET

By GIOACHINO ROSSINI

Copyright © 2019 by HAL LEONARD LLC
International Copyright Secured All Rights Reserved

HAL•LEONARD INSTRUMENTAL PLAY-ALONG

Your favorite songs are arranged just for solo instrumentalists with this outstanding series. Each book includes great full-accompaniment play-along audio so you can sound just like a pro! Check out **www.halleonard.com** to see all the titles available.

The Beatles

All You Need Is Love • Blackbird • Day Tripper • Eleanor Rigby • Get Back • Here, There and Everywhere • Hey Jude • I Will • Let It Be • Lucy in the Sky with Diamonds • Ob-La-Di, Ob-La-Da • Penny Lane • Something • Ticket to Ride • Yesterday.

______00225330 Flute $14.99
______00225331 Clarinet $14.99
______00225332 Alto Sax $14.99
______00225333 Tenor Sax $14.99
______00225334 Trumpet. $14.99
______00225335 Horn $14.99
______00225336 Trombone $14.99
______00225337 Violin. $14.99
______00225338 Viola $14.99
______00225339 Cello $14.99

Chart Hits

All About That Bass • All of Me • Happy • Radioactive • Roar • Say Something • Shake It Off • A Sky Full of Stars • Someone like You • Stay with Me • Thinking Out Loud • Uptown Funk.

______00146207 Flute $12.99
______00146208 Clarinet $12.99
______00146209 Alto Sax $12.99
______00146210 Tenor Sax $12.99
______00146211 Trumpet. $12.99
______00146212 Horn $12.99
______00146213 Trombone $12.99
______00146214 Violin. $12.99
______00146215 Viola $12.99
______00146216 Cello $12.99

Disney Greats

Arabian Nights • Hawaiian Roller Coaster Ride • It's a Small World • Look Through My Eyes • Yo Ho (A Pirate's Life for Me) • and more.

______00841934 Flute $12.99
______00841935 Clarinet $12.99
______00841936 Alto Sax $12.99
______00841937 Tenor Sax $12.95
______00841938 Trumpet. $12.99
______00841939 Horn $12.99
______00841940 Trombone $12.99
______00841941 Violin. $12.99
______00841942 Viola $12.99
______00841943 Cello $12.99
______00842078 Oboe $12.99

The Greatest Showman

Come Alive • From Now On • The Greatest Show • A Million Dreams • Never Enough • The Other Side • Rewrite the Stars • This Is Me • Tightrope.

______00277389 Flute $14.99
______00277390 Clarinet $14.99
______00277391 Alto Sax $14.99
______00277392 Tenor Sax $14.99
______00277393 Trumpet. $14.99
______00277394 Horn $14.99
______00277395 Trombone $14.99
______00277396 Violin. $14.99
______00277397 Viola $14.99
______00277398 Cello $14.99

Movie and TV Music

The Avengers • Doctor Who XI • Downton Abbey • Game of Thrones • Guardians of the Galaxy • Hawaii Five-O • Married Life • Rey's Theme (from *Star Wars: The Force Awakens*) • The X-Files • and more.

______00261807 Flute $12.99
______00261808 Clarinet $12.99
______00261809 Alto Sax $12.99
______00261810 Tenor Sax $12.99
______00261811 Trumpet. $12.99
______00261812 Horn $12.99
______00261813 Trombone $12.99
______00261814 Violin. $12.99
______00261815 Viola $12.99
______00261816 Cello $12.99

12 Pop Hits

Believer • Can't Stop the Feeling • Despacito • It Ain't Me • Look What You Made Me Do • Million Reasons • Perfect • Send My Love (To Your New Lover) • Shape of You • Slow Hands • Too Good at Goodbyes • What About Us.

______00261790 Flute $12.99
______00261791 Clarinet $12.99
______00261792 Alto Sax $12.99
______00261793 Tenor Sax $12.99
______00261794 Trumpet. $12.99
______00261795 Horn $12.99
______00261796 Trombone $12.99
______00261797 Violin. $12.99
______00261798 Viola $12.99
______00261799 Cello $12.99

Songs from Frozen, Tangled and Enchanted

Do You Want to Build a Snowman? • For the First Time in Forever • Happy Working Song • I See the Light • In Summer • Let It Go • Mother Knows Best • That's How You Know • True Love's First Kiss • When Will My Life Begin • and more.

______00126921 Flute $14.99
______00126922 Clarinet $14.99
______00126923 Alto Sax $14.99
______00126924 Tenor Sax $14.99
______00126925 Trumpet. $14.99
______00126926 Horn $14.99
______00126927 Trombone $14.99
______00126928 Violin. $14.99
______00126929 Viola $14.99
______00126930 Cello $14.99

Top Hits

Adventure of a Lifetime • Budapest • Die a Happy Man • Ex's & Oh's • Fight Song • Hello • Let It Go • Love Yourself • One Call Away • Pillowtalk • Stitches • Writing's on the Wall.

______00171073 Flute $12.99
______00171074 Clarinet $12.99
______00171075 Alto Sax $12.99
______00171106 Tenor Sax $12.99
______00171107 Trumpet. $12.99
______00171108 Horn $12.99
______00171109 Trombone $12.99
______00171110 Violin. $12.99
______00171111 Viola $12.99
______00171112 Cello $12.99

Wicked

As Long As You're Mine • Dancing Through Life • Defying Gravity • For Good • I'm Not That Girl • Popular • The Wizard and I • and more.

______00842236 Flute $12.99
______00842237 Clarinet $12.99
______00842238 Alto Saxophone $12.99
______00842239 Tenor Saxophone. $11.95
______00842240 Trumpet. $12.99
______00842241 Horn $12.99
______00842242 Trombone $12.99
______00842243 Violin. $12.99
______00842244 Viola $12.99
______00842245 Cello $12.99

Prices, contents, and availability subject to change without notice.
Disney characters and Artwork ™ & © 2018 Disney

1118
488

101 SONGS

BIG COLLECTIONS OF FAVORITE SONGS ARRANGED FOR SOLO INSTRUMENTALISTS.

101 BROADWAY SONGS

00154199	Flute	$14.99
00154200	Clarinet	$14.99
00154201	Alto Sax	$14.99
00154202	Tenor Sax	$14.99
00154203	Trumpet	$14.99
00154204	Horn	$14.99
00154205	Trombone	$14.99
00154206	Violin	$14.99
00154207	Viola	$14.99
00154208	Cello	$14.99

101 CHRISTMAS SONGS

00278637	Flute	$14.99
00278638	Clarinet	$14.99
00278639	Alto Sax	$14.99
00278640	Tenor Sax	$14.99
00278641	Trumpet	$14.99
00278642	Horn	$14.99
00278643	Trombone	$14.99
00278644	Violin	$14.99
00278645	Viola	$14.99
00278646	Cello	$14.99

101 CLASSICAL THEMES

00155315	Flute	$14.99
00155317	Clarinet	$14.99
00155318	Alto Sax	$14.99
00155319	Tenor Sax	$14.99
00155320	Trumpet	$14.99
00155321	Horn	$14.99
00155322	Trombone	$14.99
00155323	Violin	$14.99
00155324	Viola	$14.99
00155325	Cello	$14.99

101 DISNEY SONGS

00244104	Flute	$16.99
00244106	Clarinet	$16.99
00244107	Alto Sax	$16.99
00244108	Tenor Sax	$16.99
00244109	Trumpet	$16.99
00244112	Horn	$16.99
00244120	Trombone	$16.99
00244121	Violin	$16.99
00244125	Viola	$16.99
00244126	Cello	$16.99

101 HIT SONGS

00194561	Flute	$16.99
00197182	Clarinet	$16.99
00197183	Alto Sax	$16.99
00197184	Tenor Sax	$16.99
00197185	Trumpet	$16.99
00197186	Horn	$16.99
00197187	Trombone	$16.99
00197188	Violin	$16.99
00197189	Viola	$16.99
00197190	Cello	$16.99

101 JAZZ SONGS

00146363	Flute	$14.99
00146364	Clarinet	$14.99
00146366	Alto Sax	$14.99
00146367	Tenor Sax	$14.99
00146368	Trumpet	$14.99
00146369	Horn	$14.99
00146370	Trombone	$14.99
00146371	Violin	$14.99
00146372	Viola	$14.99
00146373	Cello	$14.99

101 MOVIE HITS

00158087	Flute	$14.99
00158088	Clarinet	$14.99
00158089	Alto Sax	$14.99
00158090	Tenor Sax	$14.99
00158091	Trumpet	$14.99
00158092	Horn	$14.99
00158093	Trombone	$14.99
00158094	Violin	$14.99
00158095	Viola	$14.99
00158096	Cello	$14.99

101 POPULAR SONGS

00224722	Flute	$16.99
00224723	Clarinet	$16.99
00224724	Alto Sax	$16.99
00224725	Tenor Sax	$16.99
00224726	Trumpet	$16.99
00224727	Horn	$16.99
00224728	Trombone	$16.99
00224729	Violin	$16.99
00224730	Viola	$16.99
00224731	Cello	$16.99

Prices, contents and availability subject to change without notice.

1118

101 TIPS FROM HAL LEONARD

STUFF ALL THE PROS KNOW AND USE

Ready to take your skills to the next level? These books present valuable how-to insight that musicians of all styles and levels can benefit from. The text, photos, music, diagrams and accompanying audio provide a terrific, easy-to-use resource for a variety of topics.

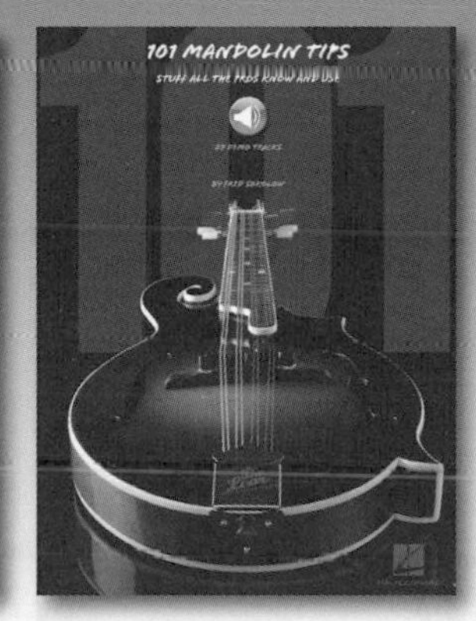

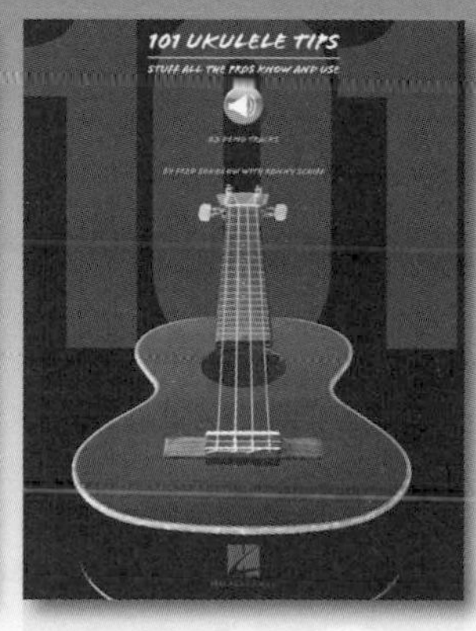

101 HAMMOND B-3 TIPS
by Brian Charette
Topics include: funky scales and modes; unconventional harmonies; creative chord voicings; cool drawbar settings; ear-grabbing special effects; professional gigging advice; practicing effectively; making good use of the pedals; and much more!
00128918 Book/Online Audio $14.99

101 HARMONICA TIPS
by Steve Cohen
Topics include: techniques, position playing, soloing, accompaniment, the blues, equipment, performance, maintenance, and much more!
00821040 Book/Online Audio $16.99

101 CELLO TIPS—2ND EDITION
by Angela Schmidt
Topics include: bowing techniques, non-classical playing, electric cellos, accessories, gig tips, practicing, recording and much more!
00149094 Book/Online Audio $14.99

101 FLUTE TIPS
by Elaine Schmidt
Topics include: selecting the right flute for you, finding the right teacher, warm-up exercises, practicing effectively, taking good care of your flute, gigging advice, staying and playing healthy, and much more.
00119883 Book/CD Pack................................$14.99

101 SAXOPHONE TIPS
by Eric Morones
Topics include: techniques; maintenance; equipment; practicing; recording; performance; and much more!
00311082 Book/CD Pack................................$15.99

101 TRUMPET TIPS
by Scott Barnard
Topics include: techniques, articulation, tone production, soloing, exercises, special effects, equipment, performance, maintenance and much more.
00312082 Book/CD Pack................................$14.99

101 UPRIGHT BASS TIPS
by Andy McKee
Topics include: right- and left-hand technique, improvising and soloing, practicing, proper care of the instrument, ear training, performance, and much more.
00102009 Book/Online Audio $14.99

101 BASS TIPS
by Gary Willis
Topics include: techniques, improvising and soloing, equipment, practicing, ear training, performance, theory, and much more.
00695542 Book/Online Audio $17.99

101 DRUM TIPS—2ND EDITION
Topics include: grooves, practicing, warming up, tuning, gear, performance, and much more!
00151936 Book/Online Audio $14.99

101 FIVE-STRING BANJO TIPS
by Fred Sokolow
Topics include: techniques, ear training, performance, and much more!
00696647 Book/CD Pack................................$14.99

101 GUITAR TIPS
by Adam St. James
Topics include: scales, music theory, truss rod adjustments, proper recording studio set-ups, and much more. The book also features snippets of advice from some of the most celebrated guitarists and producers in the music business.
00695737 Book/Online Audio $16.99

101 MANDOLIN TIPS
by Fred Sokolow
Topics include: playing tips, practicing tips, accessories, mandolin history and lore, practical music theory, and much more!
00119493 Book/Online Audio $14.99

101 RECORDING TIPS
by Adam St. James
This book contains recording tips, suggestions, and advice learned firsthand from legendary producers, engineers, and artists. These tricks of the trade will improve anyone's home or pro studio recordings.
00311035 Book/CD Pack................................$14.95

101 UKULELE TIPS
by Fred Sokolow with Ronny Schiff
Topics include: techniques, improvising and soloing, equipment, practicing, ear training, performance, uke history and lore, and much more!
00696596 Book/Online Audio $15.99

101 VIOLIN TIPS
by Angela Schmidt
Topics include: bowing techniques, non-classical playing, electric violins, accessories, gig tips, practicing, recording, and much more!
00842672 Book/CD Pack................................$14.99

Prices, contents and availability subject to change without notice.

HAL•LEONARD®

www.halleonard.com